DISCOVER HIDDEN POTENTIAL

BECAUSE YOU CAN

Table of Contents

Introduction

I want to thank you and congratulate you for downloading the book **'Discover Hidden Potential'**.

This book contains proven steps and strategies on how to harness your hidden potential to achieve your goals in life and be successful.

Here's an inescapable fact: you will need simple yet powerful methods to do it. And it's all available here. All you need to do is follow them perfectly and you will definitely find yourself in a new life, the one that you want at the end.

Uncapping individual potential is not as simple as we think. It takes a lot of time and more importantly the individual must be prepared for it. Without his/her will, it is going to be of no use. There are a lot of ways to unearth the individual's potential to the maximum so that he or she can achieve their goals. It's the thought process that matters the most.

The belief plays a bigger role than the thought process and trust is the most important thing that you will need to have if you want to succeed. The peculiar part in this is the way the individual thinks about himself or herself and let themselves push to the corners that they haven't seen yet.

Only when your back is against the wall you will either break it down or find another way to be comfortably seated on a couch. It not only involves the individual but everyone around him. And of course hard work is the most important thing that will be needed to make this all possible. This is where I would like to quote a famous saying, "Hardships are the only things that turn ordinary people into extraordinary".

In the first two chapters we are going to see about how you can harness your hidden potentials and in the rest of the chapters we will see about how to be successful in life.

Chapter 1

Productivity of your brain

Improving the productivity of your brain is the first thing that you will have to do to harness the hidden potentials of yourself. Your brain is the most important organ of your body. It is the most widely used part and yet neglected most of the times. It's not true that there is nothing that can be done by you to improve your brain productivity and brain function.

It is up to you to change your brain. The science community describes the process of changing your brain and rewriting it to suit your needs as neuroplasticity. It means that your brain is like a plastic, moldable, transformable, flexible, shapeable, pliable and resilient. You can improve your brain and strengthen it at any time of your life. Be it the early stages or the final stages. People often ask, "What should I do to improve my brain?" They generally do not like the answers to this question. There are three reasons for people not liking it. They are,

- **There is no simple formula.** People always think that there are simple methods available to enhance our brain. But it is not like that. You would think that a few puzzles a day or a magic pill can improve your brain. But it is not possible. It's not possible to improve an organ as complicated as our brain by just these methods. And if it were that simple, we would have all Einsteins and Edisons everywhere. These methods do not last for a long time and that is exactly what is needed to improve our brain.

- **We are people of habit.** We take in information automatically in an easier way or in a routine way so that it will be easier for us to understand it at that time and reproduce it whenever we want. This is not the way it should be done. We are killing our brain by doing this. We have to take in information in a creative way and let the brain process it more creatively. By this way we improve our brain, if you are going to process the information in a routine way, you are letting your brain rot.

- **Takes efforts.** Your brain has to work hard in transforming the information or the ideas into concepts. The more you practice deeper thinking, the more your brain functions and more effort is into thinking which is ultimately what is needed to make your brain work hard. When your brain is working really hard, that is when you achieve new heights.

Now, let's see a few methods to improve your brain productivity.

Do something new: If you are going on in a routine the brain is not stimulated at all, whereas when you are doing something new the brain gets to work more on that and it is highly stimulated. By doing something new your brain gets rejuvenated and that keeps you more active. This also creates new neural pathways in your brain and increases your intelligence. Simple things such as taking a new route to your work, trying out a new exercise, a new recipe for breakfast, all of this helps improving the brain productivity. Hence, say goodbye to your routine and try something new every day.

Exercise regularly: It's been scientifically proven that exercising helps in enhancing neurogenesis and helps to improve your brain function. In simple words, every time you exercise, new brain cells are created. Hence do a lot of exercise. This will definitely help you improve your brain function and your brain will thank you for it.

Train your memory: We hear people saying, "I wish I had a better memory" all the time. It is not impossible. Memorizing some of the important things like phone numbers, social security number, credit card number, etc. will definitely help your numbers. We always watch and wonder how people of our past generation have such a good memory. It's simple because they had to memorize all those important things and they didn't have the luxury of smart phones which literally do everything for us. Going old school is the best way to improve your memory.

Be curious: Be curious about everything in life. Curiosity is the single weapon that leads to great inventions and discoveries. Be curious about the day to day things that you do in your life. Get curious about the products you use, the services that are provided to you, the daily routine that you do, by doing this you are making your brain think and be creative. You might find new and easy or simple methods to do the stuff that you have been regularly doing till now. This way your brain is always active and you will be proud about what you did creatively about your day to day stuff.

Think positive: Stress and anxiety are known to be demons to everyone. They kill the existing neurons and also hinder the flow of already present neurons and in some cases stop the growth of neurons. So it's best to stop worrying too much and go with the flow. Studies have proved that positive thinking especially about your future speeds up the creation of new brain cells and dramatically reduce the levels of anxiety and stress. You would have experienced this, when you are stressful, it clouds your judgment. This is because when you are stressed, the brain is hardly active and hardly thinks about anything else and you are not able to make proper decisions. This is why people tend not to make any decisions when they are in anxiety or under stress. Living a stress free life is very important for the functioning of our brain.

Read a book: Reading is often considered as a stress and tension releasing method. It's also called as the best escapism. Studies have proved that when you are using your brain cells to imagine something, the whole brain is activated. After all, reading a book helps you imagine so much and it might make you get lost in that imaginary world. Reading is always a great way to trigger your imagination. And it is a great method to improve your brain activity as it helps you concentrate and focus the entire time on what you are reading and enhances your mood and makes you forget about almost everything else that is happening around you.

Ditch GPS and CALCULATORS: GPS has definitely made our lives easier but it has also made our brain lazier. Gone are the days when we used to use a map to locate the places that we are headed to. Studies have discovered that using maps actually helps us understand the spatial relationships which is there in our brain but hardly used nowadays.

And ditch the calculators. The simple and most effective way to keep our brain active is by doing math. And now, we have lost the habit of calculating stuff in our minds. For everything we just take out our phones or calculators and use them to do even simple calculations. So ban the calculators. Remember the good old days back in school where we were taught to use our brains for simple calculations like tables? We hardly remember those tables anymore. So resist the urge to use calculators and use the device that you were born with, your brain.

Get distracted: Distractions at the right levels are really important too. It makes your brain to be more focused and concentrated. If you want pin drop silence and you want to do something in peace, going to a coffee shop might not be the best idea. But certain studies have proved that working in those noises actually helps you focus more and gives better concentration on what you are doing. It in fact heightens your creativity and focus and therefore improves your brain.

Listening classical music: There are different mood enhancers around the world. Classical music has proved to be one of them. Some researchers go on to say that listening to classical music, actually increases the production of dopamine in our brain which results in movement, the ability to feel happy and the emotional response. These studies found that listening to classical music improves your visual attention to a great extent, and then the melodies boost our creative thinking, and also their rhythm literally improves our critical thinking.

Be bored: The best time you will ever have is the time that you will spend with yourself and your thoughts. Internet has spoiled that for us now. It has gone to the extent where people are actually scared to be alone with their thoughts anymore.

A study that was conducted recently found that people are ready to do whatever it takes not to be bored. The participants in the study could not be alone in a room for more than 15 minutes. This is what the internet has done to us. Being bored allows you to think a lot about whatever you want. It allows you to be creative.

Whereas nowadays people are so busy that they are doing whatever they are doing without knowing why they are doing what they are doing. Studies also reveal that when you don't have enough time for yourself to think, you lose the priced ability of listening to others and connecting and empathizing with others.

One task at a time: Almost all of us are under the impression that we can multitask. But the bitter truth is that by doing so, we are basically splitting the brain's power between two tasks. Many studies say that by doing so we are constantly flipping our brain from one task to another that the brain stops concentrating on either one of them. Some studies also show that multi-taskers are terrible at the multitasking even more than a normal person trying to do it one at a time.

Eat smart food: Food is important in everything that we do in our lives and for every organ in our body. The health of our brain depends on the healthy quality of the food that we intake. The foods that we intake, enter the body, then the bloodstream, then it enters the brain and it definitely affects the way we feel and think.

The foods that are generally suggested as healthy one for your brain are salmon, blueberries, avocados, caffeine, eggs, dark chocolate, whole grain, green tea and yogurt. Consuming these kinds of food is really important for your brain. At the same time avoiding certain foods are also important. Some of the foods that you should avoid include saturated fats, donuts, processed foods, turkey, fried foods and spicy foods. These foods actually slow down your productivity and your focus. So it's better to try to avoid them.

Spend time with nature and meditate: A study in the University of Michigan revealed that doing something as simple as going out for a walk among the nature and trees when compared to an urban place, increases your short term memory by 20%. That is a very significant number.

Taking a walk in nature actually helps you to feel fresh and it stimulates your senses and captures your attention dramatically with its breath taking views. It also let you to be in peace and help you think a lot and allows your brain to be filled with creativity and just enjoy the moment. This activates your brain more than the time you are solving a puzzle, and a lot more than your other exercises to increase the potential of your brain.

Meditation is also one of the best methods to activate your brain. When you want to expand your muscles, you exercise. The same way when you want to expand your brain you have to meditate. A recent study done at Harvard has proven that meditation helps increasing the size of your brain regions that are linked with deep thought, memory and focused attention. The study also mentions that meditation can reduce anxiety, depression, anger and fear at great levels.

Write it down: Always have the habits of writing things down. Even if it is as simple as your to do list. Studies prove that by writing things down, you don't just improve your memory but it also creates oxygenated blood flow to the parts of your brain that can help you in improving your memory. And it will also make you remember them more accurately when you write down anything. It is as simple as this, the more your brain thinks about stuff that you have actually written down, the more it becomes easier for the brain to retrieve it as it is stored as a visual memory.

Take a nap: Rest is something that is absolutely necessary if you want your brain to function properly. That is why everyone suggests you have a continued sleep for at least 6 hours a day. By that time your body will feel fresh and your brain too. And since many people do not get enough time for sleep, naps are definitely a compulsory for them. And many studies have proved that naps actually help in improving the performance of the brain. Let me give you a breakdown of naps that will be helpful for different activities.

▶ *10 to 20 minute nap- It enhances your alertness and focus for two hours.*

▶ *60 minute nap- Helps you improve your memory and learning*

▶ *90 minute nap- Increase in creativity, performance, alertness, learning, memory. A 90 minute nap does everything because that is the exact time required for your brain to experience a complete sleep cycle.*

There are definitely a lot of things that can be done to improve your brain. It's definitely not like the saying, "An old dog can never learn a new trick". If you want a much better brain, you will have to do the right stimulation which helps in the formation of new neural pathways in your brain which will automatically increase your cognitive abilities and also improves your memory power and your ability to learn and understand things better.

If you enjoyed this book, please take the time to share your thoughts and post a review on Amazon. It'd be greatly appreciated!

Chapter 2

Mind Mapping

Mind mapping is a technique by which you capture your thought and bring it to life in visual form. Mind mapping helps you to be more creative, solve problems more easily, and remember more. Mind mapping is also very useful in untapping hidden potentials. Let's have a look at it in detail.

Mind Map: A mind map is a picture that gives all the information about everything around a central object. Well consider it as a tree, more in a radial way. Basically, the main idea is at the centre and everything related to it are like branches. For example, if book is at the centre, then genres, poetry, author, number of pages, etc., are all the branches that can be connected together.

Mind maps can be used for almost any task. It can be used for even the simplest of things like learning to ride a bike, something like planning a trip, planning your career, achieving goals, etc. Nowadays there are a lot of softwares through which you can create your mind map. The Asian Efficiency Blog have used mind mapping techniques in different unique ways. Some of them are to create a knowledge bank (the files and links are attached through the software), create book summaries, solve problems (related to credit cards), etc. This kind of mind mapping is of great use for teams also. They can use it for group brainstorming, and many interactive sessions and presentations too.

Mind mapping is better than text note: There are a number of reasons why mind mapping is better than other note taking techniques. Let's have a look at some of them.

> ▶ Mind mapping is a graphical tool. Hence, it will have a variety of options to choose from words, numbers, images and colors.

Hence it will be more creative and fun to create a mind map. It is also proved that the combination of words and pictures is 6 times more effective than words alone to remember any information.

▶ Mind map helps you to find the link between each topic and the neutral element. This makes you think more about the links between the topic and the neutral element and also it helps you to find out what you are missing in case if you don't get the link.

▶ Just a quick glance of your mind map will give you the whole idea of what the subject is and it also gives you a lot of other useful information too. By just looking at it you will remember everything. Right from the main subject and how all the other topics are linked as well.

▶ It's also an interesting way of arranging our thoughts. Well it almost depicts our brain as we are always consumed with overlapping thoughts and not linear ones. This way we can relate more to the mind maps and be clearer about our thoughts.

▶ You can always generate more ideas from this method, and this tool also makes you think from different angles and takes you in different pathways. This encourages us to think out of the box and enhances our brain and the hidden potential in it very well.

In one of the surveys conducted recently, it was seen that people who used mind map software were more effective in their work and could easily see through the complicated projects they had using mind map. And researches also suggest that mind mapping increases our brain capacity and memory power by 10 to 15% when compared with the conventional method of note taking and studying. And also it saves a lot of time.

Just to give an example, let's just assume that we are taking a rock as the centre of a mind map. Immediately everyone will start writing about buildings, fossils, history, etc. But it can be used as a paperweight, or to support something which is falling down, it can be thought as a diamond, etc.

There are infinite numbers of ways to look at an object. But nowadays we blame time that we are not able to think. Mind map helps you to look at an object from every side. This stimulates your brain drastically. It improves your brain function enormously and also enhances your memory power. Hence this is one of the best methods to untap your hidden potential.

Chapter 3

Personal Development

Personal development.... What is personal development? People ponder over it so much that they finally stop thinking about it and just go on with their routine. Personally, I feel personal development is about making yourself better. It includes so many aspects.

It's not just about making more money and living a luxurious life. Of course it might be a part of it but that's not the whole part. It's also about being a good citizen, respecting people, women in particular, doing whatever it takes for your family, making your loved ones happy, spending time with people you care, having fun with your friends, making time for those who matter the most in spite of your busy schedule.

It is all about changing yourself for your own self and definitely for the greater good. Some want to change for their loved ones, some for their kids and some for their family. That is human nature. If you want to improve yourself and be successful, find out what your strength is, work hard on that. Keep working hard, success will be at your doorstep one day. But don't give up without trying hard or at least without knowing that you have done everything you can.

I would like to quote one of my favorite TV shows here. It's from suits, "What do you do when someone has a gun to your head? You either surrender or they are going to shoot you.... No, you point a bigger gun at them...." So make sure that you have exhausted your ammunition before giving up. Because giving up definitely doesn't fall in the category of Personal Development.

"Be the change you want to see in the world."

Personal development also lies in different things. Example, helping the society. Make a path of your own where people will follow your footsteps. It need not be a great revolution but a simple help like taking an old lady by her hand and help her cross the road. It's not about how big the help is, but about how useful it is. It's the small things that matter the most.

Personal development is also about self-confidence, one of the biggest things any person needs in life. You should be confident in what you do in life. Never ever underestimate yourself. And never ever let someone else tell you what you can do and what you cannot do. And your confidence builds when you are making progress.

So making progress is really important. No matter how small the progress maybe, but make sure that there is progress. And like everything in life, where there is a positive thing, there has to be a negative thing. The same way, here, it's overconfidence. Overconfidence is a big hurdle for personal development. The sooner you overcome it, the better your life will be.

"No matter how slow you go: you are still lapping everybody on the couch."

Personal Development is about improving your strengths and talents too. Finding out your strength is the most important thing in this process. Then working hard on it and working hard to improve it, is more important. Talent is considered as the big word. We all have so many talents in us. Some we know of and others hidden. Find out your talents.

You have to experiment with yourself for that. Find out the talents you have. Focus on which is the most important for you and with which you want to succeed in your life. Focus completely on that. You have to be patient. Try all possible ways to develop it.

Take someone's help if you want to, but make sure you are good at it if you are not the best. Talent needs to be groomed. So success will obviously take time but you have to be patient and never give up easily. Again confidence plays a big role here. You have to be confident and back yourself until you fail. But don't give up there too, get up and fight back.

"If you don't go after what you want, you'll never have anything."

Personal development is also about handling stress. Handling stress is very important. This is where people lose it and go down the wrong roads. Some even go psychic. Stress is always caused because of your own doings. Not meeting deadlines which you were supposed to meet, not finishing something that you started, not spending enough time on things which you have to, etc. Avoid facing situations like that. So you have to be well prepared and well in advance in everything.

Financial stability is also one of the aspects of personal development. It is very important for your future and the future of the people who are depending on you. Financial stability cannot be achieved easily. It takes a lot of time for one and forever for some. You need not have to be rich but make sure you are not poor. Learn to spend your earnings. Try to save a little bit too. It will be of help for you in the future.

Work–life balance is an art which you need to know if you want to improve yourself. Working hard for long hours is not bad but don't become a slave to your work. There are other things that you have to do in your life. Spend time with your family, this is very important. After all family is the one that is going to be with you no matter who you are, forever. Make time for people who make time for you. They are definitely worth your time. Have some recreation too. Work is not everything in life though it pays the bills. Take time to enjoy life too. Spend time on your hobbies. It helps in improving yourself a lot.

Knowledge is something that you have to improve every day. It may be related to your work or in general. But keep improving your knowledge. Be up to date with current affairs. Read a lot of newspapers, it helps a lot. Test your knowledge every day. Read a lot of books. A book is a man's best friend; it is the best companion too wherever you go. A simple conversation with wise people can be a knowledgeable experience.

"The expert in anything was once a beginner."

Personal development is definitely a lifelong process. You have keep developing and improving yourself day in and day out, find out your skills, and work hard on them to achieve success. If you want your tomorrow to be better than today, then keep developing yourself every day.

If you enjoyed this book, please take the time to share your thoughts and post a review on Amazon. It'd be greatly appreciated!

Chapter 4

Easy steps to create lasting changes

DREAM; the biggest word when it comes to achieving something or being successful. That doesn't mean that every dream should be towards achieving something or being successful. But a dream is the start to all of it. There is a famous quote, "Dreams shouldn't be the ones which makes you sleep every night but they should be the ones which keep you awake all the time". Dream big; work hard on the same. It's your dream; don't let anyone else influence it. This is the first step towards making a change and in turn progress.

"Don't let your dreams just be dreams."

PROGRESS can be defined as the change from today's reality and yesterday's. Make sure there is a slight change, little progress on each day towards your goal. Take baby steps but don't pile on your work. And the opposite to progress is postponement. Always remember "Tomorrow never comes". Progress can be easily measured, if your today is better than yesterday then you have definitely made progress.

Establishing your IDENTITY is very important to create a change. Wherever you are, how small or big your circle is, whomever you are working with they have to know you. They have to know what you do, what you are capable of. Create an identity for yourself. Respect people around you and be respected. Having an identity is a key to achieve whatever it is that you want.

Once you establish your identity then it's the reputation that comes with it. Make sure you live up to it. Maintaining your reputation involves your character, attitude etc. You should know when to show your attitude and when not to. Attitude makes all the difference.

Showing the right attitude at the right place can take you a long distance.

When we talk about attitude the one thing that comes with it are EMOTONS. Managing emotions is an art for a few and a thorn for a few. The man who has control on his emotions has complete control over his life. Everyone is emotional but you should know where to show it. Some people exploit it as your weakness, beware, if it is your weakness, learn how to turn it into one of your strengths. You have to control all your emotions and frustrations to get to where you want to. It can be difficult and it will definitely take time but make sure people don't get the better of you because of it.

INTERPERSONAL RELATOINSHIPS matter a lot when you want to create lasting changes in your life. It's your life, reality is the biggest teacher. Every relationship matters. There will definitely be something that you can learn from each and every one of them. It's easily the best example not to make the same mistake twice. But it does happen; see the positives in that too. There is a lesson to be learnt in all of them. And more importantly stay positive and steer clear of people who are not.

CHOICES, they change your life drastically. Make new choices for yourself rather than letting your old choices make it for you. Embrace your new choice, go with it and make sure you have made the right choice. If not, start over, there is always a second chance. But be sure about the choices you make, because in certain things, the second chance is not always your option. And before making a new choice, think if that is what you want for yourself and for your future. Never ever settle down for something less when you deserve more.

TALK TO YOURSELF, this is very important. You are your own best friend. Make it an everyday habit. It will make you realize who you actually are and what are you doing and is it really worthy doing all this and where will you be in a few years from now. You might not have someone to go to, so talking to yourself is definitely the best thing you can do at times like that. If you do have someone then talk to them, share everything with them, speak out. It is necessary. Another way is to write. Write down everything you feel. All your emotions, frustrations, everything. It helps you a lot. Then think what you can do improve all of them.

Be POSITIVE. This is one of the basic qualities you should possess. If not develop it. It's the most essential quality you need to have to create a lasting change in your life. Think positively in whatever you do. Avoid negative thoughts and negative people. Be with those who think positively about you and want something good for you. Positive thoughts come when your mind is fresh, so keep your mind fresh always.

STRESS MANAGEMENT. It's the biggest thing that you have to follow to create a lasting change in yourself. There are so many ways to manage stress. Make time for your hobbies, listen to music, dance your heart out, have a drink (not just beer, maybe a coffee or tea too). Make time for those things from which you get pleasure and you are happy doing those things. Some people might need a punch bag and some might need a shooting range. It's your wish, but don't let the stress get to you. It has caused so many suicides, so many have gone psychic and some into depression. When you are under stress, your performance level also goes down. You don't work in the way you used to and everything goes south then. So make sure you don't put yourself under any unwanted stress. You can even use the help of psychiatrists on this matter if you can't manage it on your own.

CONTROL YOUR ADDICTIONS. This is when things go south ways. You need to learn to control your addictions, if you can't do it on your own; there are help centers readily available. I'm not saying to quit anything or give up whatever your addiction is. But you need to have it under control. You should be able to be free of it when required. One of the ways to control your addiction is not to think about it. Try to stay away for a few days from it or the people who do it. It's all about your mind. Control your mind and you can control everything.

SIMPLIFICATION, simplify whatever you can, whenever you can. Keep things simple. When it gets complicated that's when the problems come calling. Don't stack up everything till the last minute. It depends on you how to simplify things. Have a planned timetable; make sure you are not lagging behind. It's really easy when you finish things then and there.

This definitely brings us to TIME MANAGEMENT. This is where most people fail as they don't know to manage their time. If you are a lazy person, you'll remain one forever. In that case, set a deadline date one day before the actual day. And I'm not saying that you can't be lazy, after all the lazy ones are the ones who think of new methods to finish off their work fast. But time management is a whole new concept.

You need to be weary of every minute. Especially when you have a deadline. This will take a long time, because we never finish anything fast until our ass is on fire. So it's very important that you preplan everything that you have and make the most of your time every day. These are some of the simple rituals to create lasting changes. Give it a try.

Chapter 5

Achieve your goals

The first step towards achieving your goal is setting them. Always aim higher. That's the attitude you need to have when you are going to set your goals. Make sure that you aim one step ahead of what you want so that even if you fail at the last one, you have already succeeded in achieving whatever you wanted. While you are at it, use this technique. The goals which you are going to set for yourself must be SMART. Smart is abbreviated here. It stands for,

S – Specific

M – Measurable

A – Attainable

R – Relevant

T – Time bound

You have to be very specific when it comes to setting your goals. You have to exactly know what is it that you are trying to achieve. It must be very precise. Never use the words "some" or "little bit" or "maybe" when you are setting your goals, because that itself shows that you are not going to accomplish it. You can accomplish anything only when you precisely know what it is that you want to accomplish. Clear your head make sure that you want something and you are going do it no matter what, and then set your goal knowing that you can achieve it.

How do you measure your goals?? It's by the everyday improvement. That's how you measure your goals. If you don't measure your goal, then it will just be a forever dream. Check the progress that you have done towards your goal every day. Every step is important and make sure that you are going in the right direction.

Think before every move you make and then proceed. For example, if your goal is to lose 10 pounds in a week, then check if you have at least lost one and half a pound every day. This is how you measure your goal.

Your goals should be attainable. It should be attainable according to your own standards. Set the benchmark for yourself. Unattainable goals are just dreams. They are of no help when you want to achieve your real goal. It should be practical according to you. That doesn't mean you can't aim for something which you are not meant for. I'm a strong believer in "Nothing is impossible".

Be very sure that whatever your goal is, you clearly know that it can be attained. An example of unattainable goal is, wanting to go the moon. Yes, a few have done it, but can you do it? Do you have it in you? That's the question you have to ask yourself. So set goals which are theoretically possible for you to accomplish them.

"A goal without a plan is just a wish."

Have relevant goals in your life. Listen to your heart. Do whatever you want in life. It's your life; you have to decide for yourself. Otherwise you wouldn't want to achieve the goal and it will just be a halfhearted effort and then you will blame someone else for all of it. Thus making the goal totally irrelevant to you and in the end all that you will be left with in your life are regrets, for example, trying to become a doctor just because your father is a doctor. If you are interested in it, then go ahead. But don't do it for someone's sake, after all it's your life. Live it to the maximum.

"You can't have a million-dollar dream with a minimum wage work ethic."

Setting your goal to a certain period of time is very important. You have to set a deadline for yourself and make sure you race to the finish line rather than taking it like a stroll in the park. Time is everything in life. Or it can be said, time is money and time flies.

You will never get back your yesterday and tomorrow will never come. So make use of every second of today to the maximum. Setting a deadline, will tell you what to do within a period of time and what you should have done within a certain period of time and also what you have not done within that time period. Hence setting a deadline is always important.

Your goals should also be STRATEGIC. Set a goal that is going to help you in many aspects of your life. Like if you multitask, the goal also must be multi rewarding. When you are going to work so hard to achieve it, make sure it is worth it. For example, if your goal is to run a 10k race, it is going to help you in a different number of ways like, you will feel great about it, you can lose your weight, you can lower your cholesterol level, it strengthens your heart, increases your energy and stamina, etc. Set goals that help you out in a lot of ways. That is the whole point. Another example is, if you are going to work a job, make sure it pays you well for your own expenses, insurance for your health and for your family members and also other allowances.

"If you always do what you have always done,

You will always get what you have always gotten."

WRITE down your goals. When you write down your goals, you get more clarity of it. It makes you think in different ways like, is it the right time to go for it? What are all the things that I should prepare myself with to achieve this goal? Can I achieve it in the way I want? etc. This clarity helps you to go on with it or drop this goal and take up another. And stick it on your fridge or in the mirror or someplace that you see every day.

This helps you in focusing and it constantly keeps reminding you that you have to do this to achieve your goal. So writing it down is very important and make sure you have written it precisely.

BREAK DOWN your goal into smaller pieces so that it becomes easy to achieve them. When you look at your goal, it might look like a daunting task, but break it down to chunks, it looks a lot easier. Break them down according to the time available for you or the amount of work that you have to do every day, it becomes a lot easier. Or break it down according to the process of it, and setting a time period for each process. Rome wasn't built in one day. Nothing in this world can be achieved in a day, so take one step at a time and go about it and you'll definitely achieve it easily.

"While you have been waiting to find the easy way or the perfect time,

Someone else is already working hard to get results

Because they have decided that making progress is more important than making excuses."

BRAINSTORM new ideas. Think of different possible ways to achieve your goal. Write down the ideas that come to your mind. However small, ridiculous or impossible it is. Think from different angles on how to achieve your goal. Visualize your goals. It's as simple as picturing yourself right now and where you are according to your plan or goal and what are the things that you have to do to attain your goal and if you are on the right path.

There will be many possible ways through which you can achieve your goal, choose the best and the one in which you feel more comfortable. Don't choose a way just because it's the easiest; choose one which you know that will help you achieve your goal in the best way. Having more ideas and having options always helps.

SEEK HELP. If you can't achieve your goal on your own, ask for help. There is nothing wrong in asking someone's help but make sure you don't forget them or let them down. Sometimes you can't achieve everything on your own, you'll definitely need help, at that time, don't hesitate. Take it.

Ask from people who are already experienced in it and have done something similar to it so that they can guide you in the right way. Experience always matters so it's better to ask someone who is experienced. Because they will know the problems that you might face and will be ready to help you out through them.

LEARN FROM YOUR MISTAKES. To err is human, to forgive Divine. We all make mistakes, but learn from them. Don't repeat them. Mistakes always happen because of carelessness. So don't be careless. It also happens when you are in urgency or desperate for something. That is why you have to finish a day's work in the same day. Mistakes are part and parcel of life. Achieving your goal, is a long process, so naturally you will make mistakes but make sure they are small, not a blunder, and make sure that you can correct them and move on and not lose much time on it.

Your goal should be righteous. It shouldn't be illegal or unethical. Your thoughts should be clear and right. Because when you are doing something wrong, you will realize that it is wrong and it will pave way for mistakes and ultimately you won't feel like doing it, which is good by the way. You wouldn't want to do something wrong unless you are desperate for something. So don't put yourself in that position. Try to avoid it as early as possible. And even if you are in a desperate state, it does not give you the right to do something that is illegal or unethical.

All of this can simply be put as,

"It had long since come to my attention that people of accomplishment rarely sat back and let things happen to them. They went out and happened to things." - Leonardo da Vinci

"When obstacles arise, you change your direction to reach your goal; you do not change your decision to get there."

Conclusion

Thank you again for downloading this book!

I hope this book was able to help you with whatever you wanted to know about harnessing untapped potentials and to achieve success in your life. Being successful is just not enough. You have to be happy about it. Be content with it. A few more things that you have to do to be happy and successful are just mentioned here.

The next step is to LIVE THE MOMENT. You have worked hard to deserve it in your life. So embrace it, enjoy it. Don't take too much time in that also, because your next goal might be starting from the next day itself. That moment, you never know if it's going to come back, so have the maximum fun. That's the moment, when you feel that you are the king of the world. Also, share it with people who were responsible for it, with the ones who are your life. But don't get too lost.

BE PASSIONATE. Always be passionate about something. Because, that is what that keeps us going. That allows us to set our next goals and that is the main thing that makes us feel so happy when we have achieved success. Passion is everything. That is what we are supposed to live for, isn't it?

Passion is different for different people. For some, their work will be their passion, for some work is different and their passion is different. At times like that, make sure that you have enough time for both and that one does not affect the other. You can't always make your passion as your career choice for various reasons, so make sure you crave out time for the things that you are passionate about in life, so that you enjoy your life. So always be passionate about something or the other.

OVERCONFIDENCE is the biggest demon when you have achieved success. If you don't want to lose yourself in the success you have achieved, then you will have to keep your overconfidence IN CHECK. Never forget all the hard work that you have put in to get where you are right now might just vanish because of one stupid move. Don't be too tempted towards unwanted things. When you are overconfident, things like this will happen, make sure you can control the urge towards them.

Don't GAMBLE with your success. If you have succeeded once, it doesn't mean that you are going to be successful all the times. So don't ever gamble with your success at stake. Always remember, climbing down is very easy but going to the top is what matters and you very well know how difficult it is as you have done it once.

Remember things that you are GRATEFUL for. And remember the people who gave you those things. Share your success with them. Obviously they wouldn't be expecting it but would it have been possible without them? So take some time out for them too. Always make room for happiness. And always spread it to your loved ones. There is nothing more contagious than a smile. So keep smiling and make others smile too.

Once you have achieved success, that doesn't mean that it's going to last forever. So don't take anything for GRANTED. Be thankful for it and make sure that you work hard as you did to keep achieving it again and again.

Come on, you have worked so hard to achieve your goal, just go enjoy it with a beer and with the people you want to have it with. That's the way to go.

Finally, if you enjoyed this book, please take the time to share your thoughts and post a review on Amazon. It'd be greatly appreciated!

Thank you and good luck!

www.ingramcontent.com/pod-product-compliance
Lightning Source LLC
Chambersburg PA
CBHW071323280526
45788CB00004B/1996